10 Left-Handed Improvisational Etudes For Saxophone

By Jeff Coffin

Artwork by Jeff Coffin.
Back Cover Photo by Rodrigo Simas.
Book layout and engraving by Kyle Gordon.

ISBN: 978-1-953622-17-4

Also available as an e-book.
www.jeffcoffin.com/LHetudes

10 LEFT-HANDED IMPROVISATIONAL ETUDES FOR SAXOPHONE

by Jeff Coffin

How (and why?!?) did this all come about? A few years back, during a practice session, I decided to challenge myself by playing ONLY with my left hand. I made a couple of videos and kind of left it at that (no pun intended), but it was always in the back of my mind to go further with it. I had witnessed pianists like Phineas Newborn Jr., and others (as well as numerous classical pianists) play solos with only their left hands and I thought, if they can do it, so can I! I discovered it wasn't quite as easy as it sounded. Cause it sounds kinda easy, right??

All of these etudes are improvisations over jazz standards. I played through them a number of times using iReal Pro as the backing track, and once I was ok with what I had played, I transcribed each solo. I changed a few little things here and there to make the etudes a little more clear, or to clean up some of the notes I didn't necessarily mean to play. I absolutely blame my right hand for not helping out more!!

All my books are meant to benefit not only my current students but also the many students I have worked with over the years. I find there are certain fundamental aspects of the saxophone that usually need to be addressed and I have tried to address those various fundamentals in my books.

Playing these particular etudes on saxophone has many benefits. They help in 'voicing' the notes more naturally and consistently. They also help with intonation, phrasing, voice leading, melody, rhythm, time, interval leaps, harmonic and rhythmic displacement, pattern recognition (sight reading), and more.

To play these, you have to relax and sort of let your body take over the process. They aren't easy but they are certainly not unplayable. Most importantly, you're gonna learn some things and they are fun to play! They are not meant to be played too quickly so take your time and really hear the phrases. I always recommend playing things slowly at first, that is to say, REALLY SLOWLY. Getting the lines clean and making them feel as smooth and consistent as possible is the goal.

I first played these on tenor sax so, if you play them on alto be sure to transpose your backing track. You should play along using the iReal Pro app, because that's what I used when I played and recorded these. You can download a recording of me playing each of these etudes (on tenor and alto sax) on my website at www.jeffcoffin.com/lhetudes

You will notice that there are many 'fourth line D' notes in these etudes. For clarity, I am using side D (Palm D). I was tempted to use side Eb (Palm Eb), and altissimo, but avoided both because I felt that doing so would overcomplicate these already complicated etudes.

So here it is, my book of Left-Handed Improvisational Etudes for your educational edification. I truly believe these will help musicians of all levels take their saxophone playing to an entirely new level. I certainly noticed a number of things in my own playing that were helped by doing these. Thanks so much for checking these out and please let me know what you think of them. Peace, JC

–

Great idea for an etude book. You could even cook breakfast with your right hand while playing these! - **BOB MINTZER**

Jeff has created an amazing group of etudes. Highly recommended! - **TONY DAGRADI**

Challenging and fun etudes that stump the left hand and explore the extremes of the horn.
- **BOB SHEPPARD**

Jeff's Left Hand Etudes are so much fun! What more could you ask for?!? - **ROXY COSS**

It's always fun to find new and interesting ways to practice your instrument! You can add this to your arsenal! - **BILL EVANS**

If you're looking for a source of fresh material to master on the saxophone - you'll find it here. Highly recommended! - **JOEL FRAHM**

Check 'em out and be ready to shed! - **DON ALIQUO**

10 LEFT-HANDED IMPROVISATIONAL ETUDES FOR SAXOPHONE

ALL THE THINGS YOU ARE

JEFF COFFIN

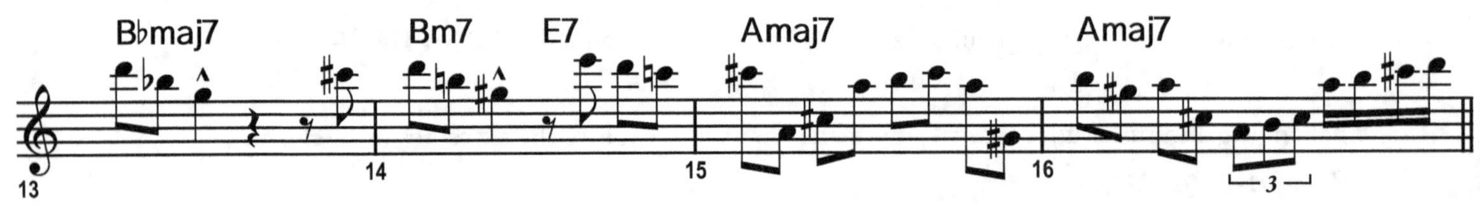

D
Gm7
Cm7
F7
B♭maj7
25
26
27
28
E♭maj7
E♭m7
Dm7
D♭°7
29
30
31
32

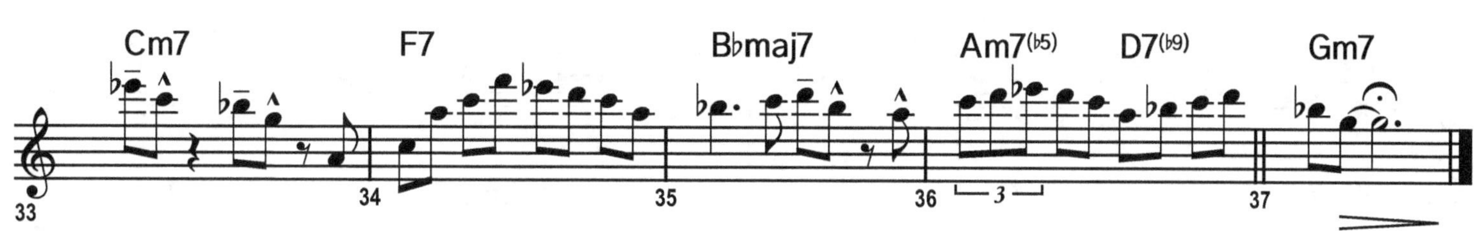
Cm7
F7
B♭maj7
Am7(♭5)
D7(♭9)
Gm7
33
34
35
36
3
37

AUTUMN LEAVES

JEFF COFFIN

DON'T CONFUSE ACTIVITY WITH PROGRESS

10 LEFT-HANDED IMPROVISATIONAL ETUDES FOR SAXOPHONE

BLUES

JEFF COFFIN

C7
A7
Dm7
19
20
21
3

G7
C7
G7
22
23
24
3

C
C7
F7
C7
25
26
27

C7
F7
F7
28
29
30
3
3

C7
A7
Dm7
31
32
33

G7
C7
G7
C7
34
35
36
37
3
3
3

CHEROKEE

JEFF COFFIN

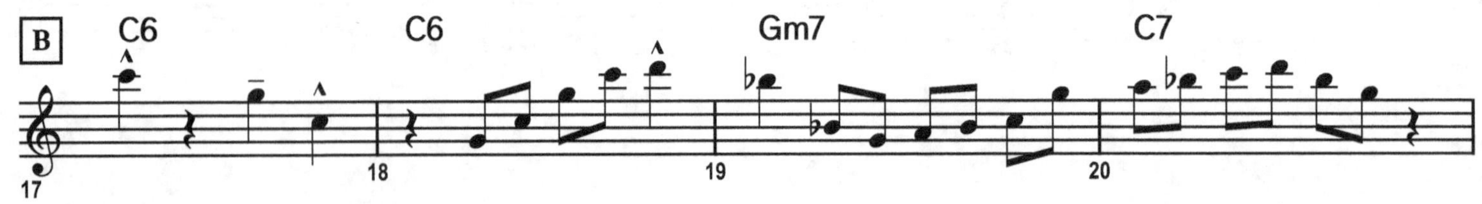

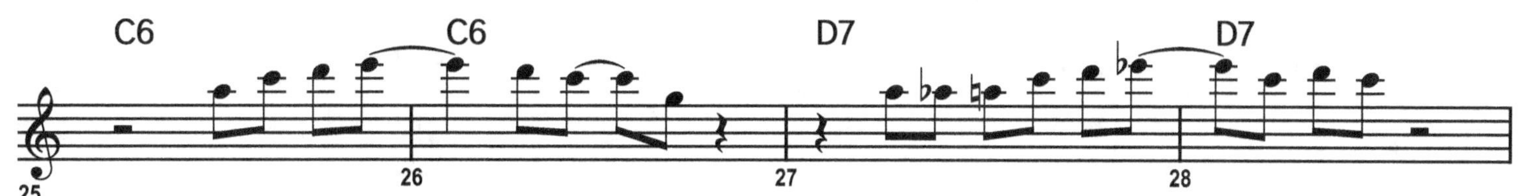
C6
C6
D7
D7
25
26
27
28

Dm7
G7
C6
C6
29
30
31
32

C
E♭m7
A♭7
D♭maj7
D♭maj7
33
34
35
36

C♯m7
F♯7
Bmaj7
Bmaj7
3
37
38
39
40

Bm7
E7
A6
Amaj7
41
42
43
44

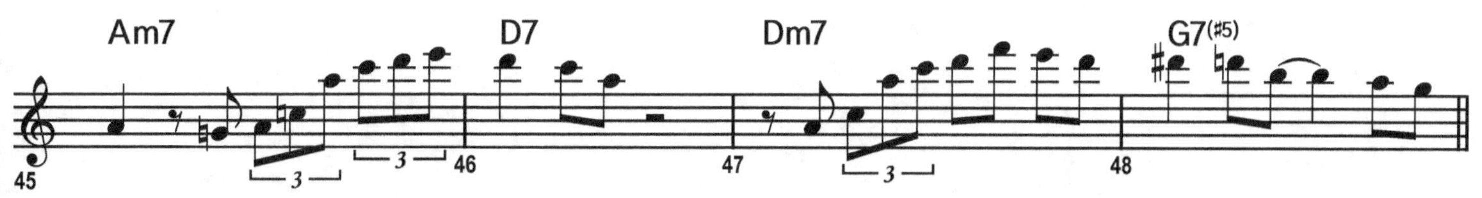
Am7
D7
Dm7
G7(♯5)
3
3
3
45
46
47
48

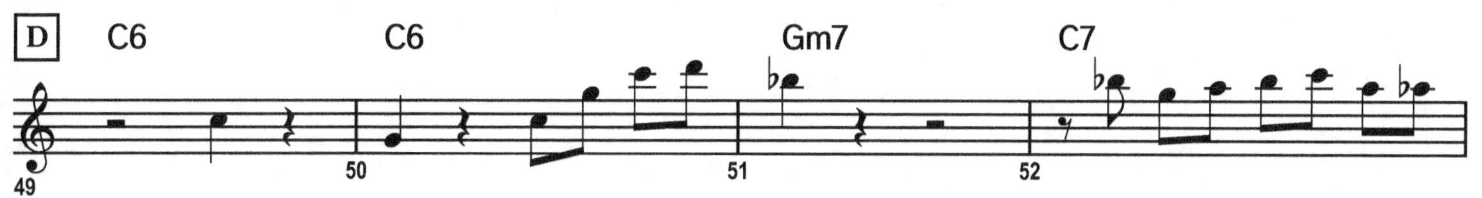
D
C6
C6
Gm7
C7
49
50
51
52

Fmaj7
Fmaj7
B♭7
B♭7
53
54
55
56
C6
C6
D7
D7
57
58
59
60
Dm7
G7
C6
C6
C6
61
62
63
64
65

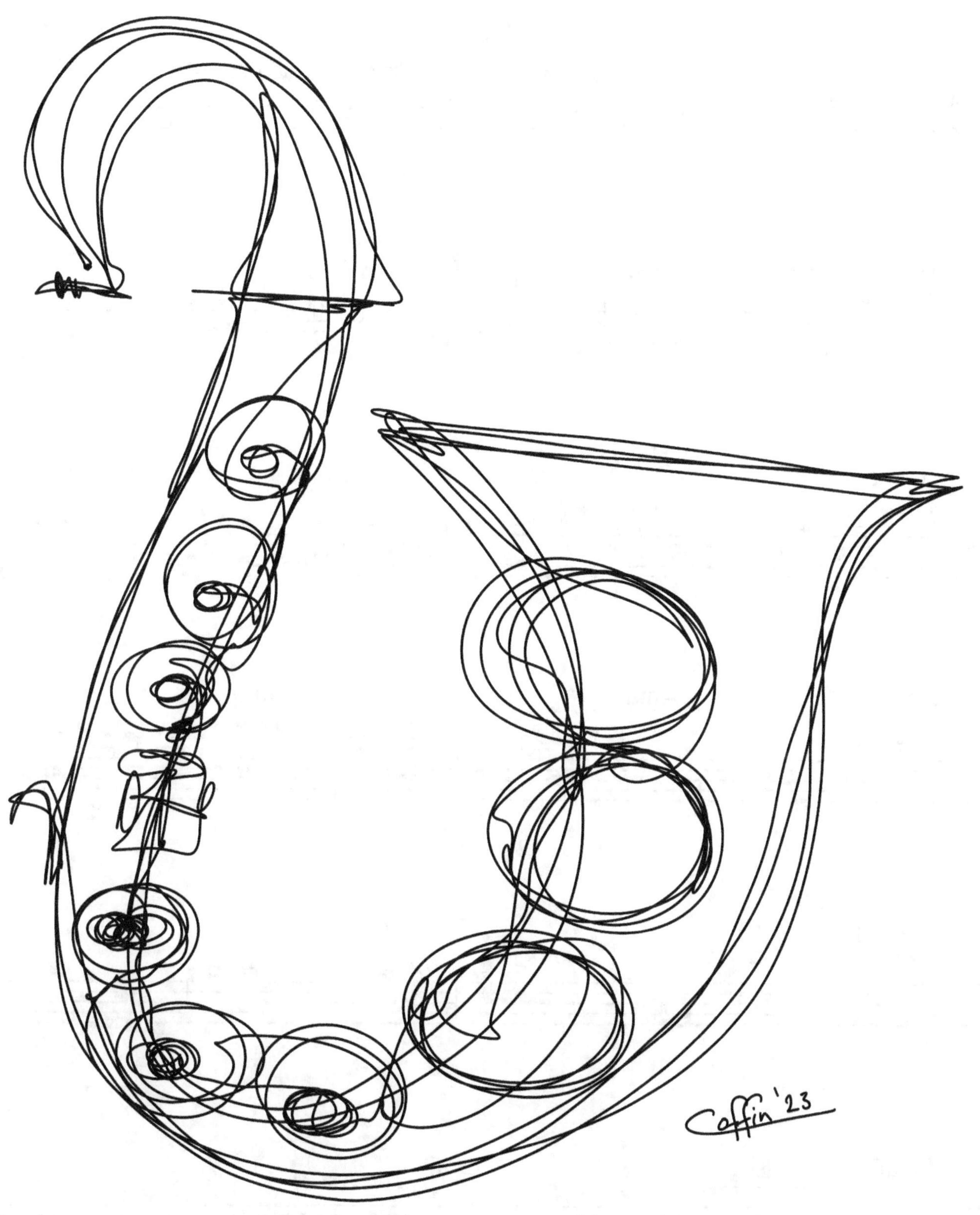
Coffin '23

10 LEFT-HANDED IMPROVISATIONAL ETUDES FOR SAXOPHONE

GIANT STEPS

JEFF COFFIN

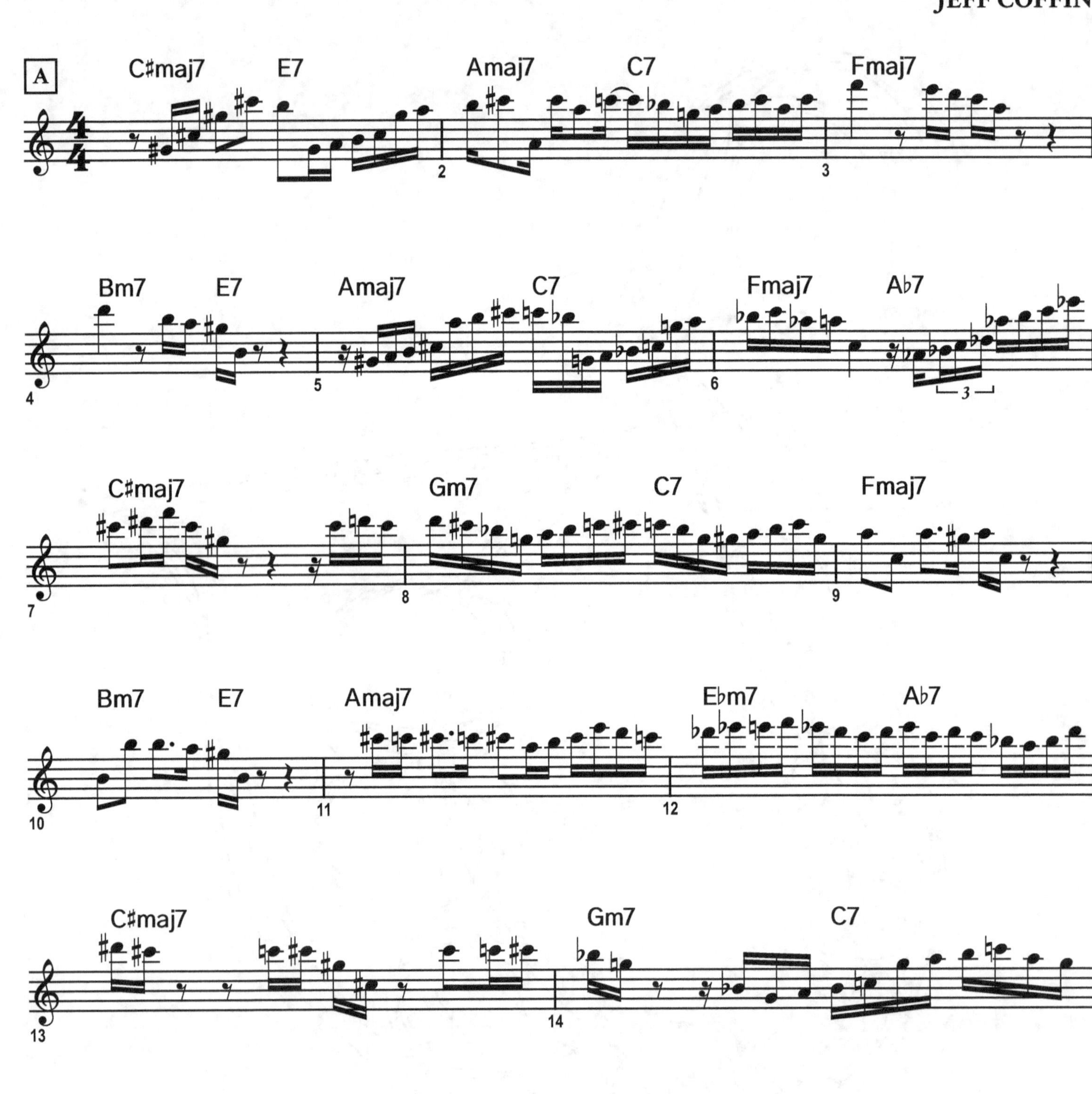

B
C#maj7
E7
Amaj7
C7
Fmaj7
Bm7
E7
Amaj7
C7
Fmaj7 A♭7
3
C#maj7
Gm7
C7
Fmaj7
Bm7
E7
Amaj7
E♭m7
A♭7
C#
Gm7
C7
Fmaj7
E♭m7
A♭7
C#maj7
E7
17
18
19
20
21
22
23
24
25
26
27
28
29
30
31
32
33

JOY SPRING

JEFF COFFIN

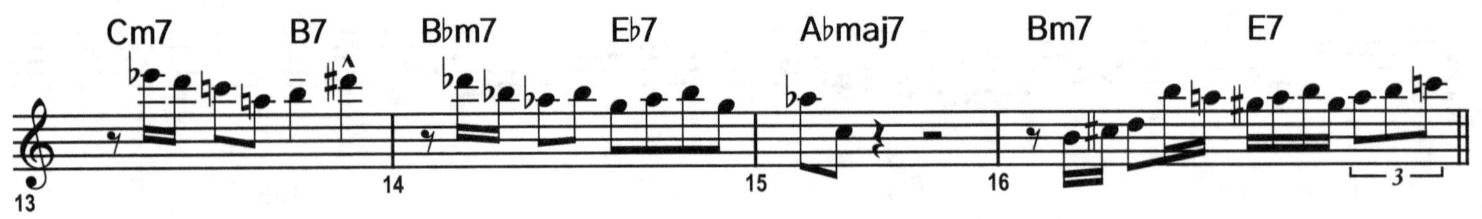

D
Gmaj7
Am7
D7
Gmaj7
Cm7
F7
25
26
27
28
3

Bm7
B♭7
G♯○
Am7
D7
Gmaj7
Am7 D7
29
30
31
32

E
Gmaj7
Am7
D7
Gmaj7
Cm7
F7
33
34
35
36
3

Bm7
B♭7
Am7
D7
Gmaj7
B♭m7
E♭7
37
38
39
40

F
A♭maj7
B♭m7
E♭7
A♭maj7
C♯m7
F♯7
41
42
43
44
3

Cm7
B7
B♭m7
E♭7
A♭maj7
Bm7
E7
45
46
47
48

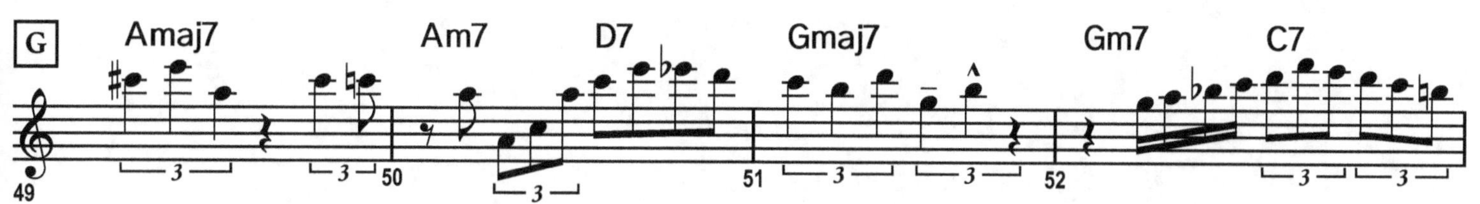
G
Amaj7
Am7
D7
Gmaj7
Gm7
C7
49
50
51
52
3

Fmaj7
B♭m7
E♭7
A♭maj7
Am7
D7
53
54
55
56

H
Gmaj7
Am7
D7
Gmaj7
Cm7
F7
57
58
59
60

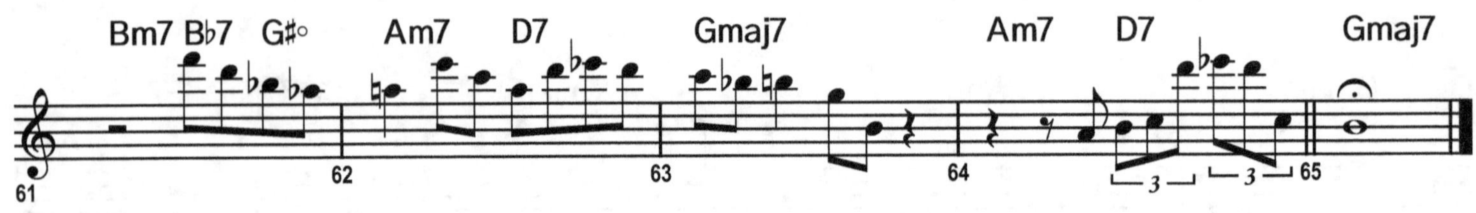
Bm7 B♭7 G♯○
Am7
D7
Gmaj7
Am7
D7
Gmaj7
61
62
63
64
65

—

The Big Five Fundamentals

—

Listening

Tone / Dynamics

Articulation

Rhythm / Time

Harmony

10 LEFT-HANDED IMPROVISATIONAL ETUDES FOR SAXOPHONE

JUST FRIENDS

JEFF COFFIN

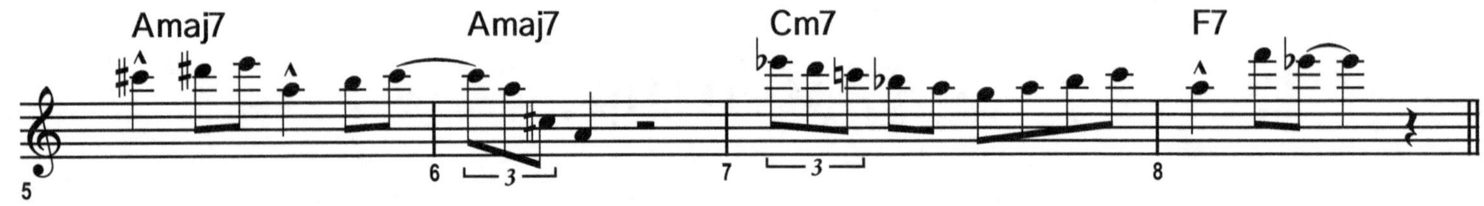

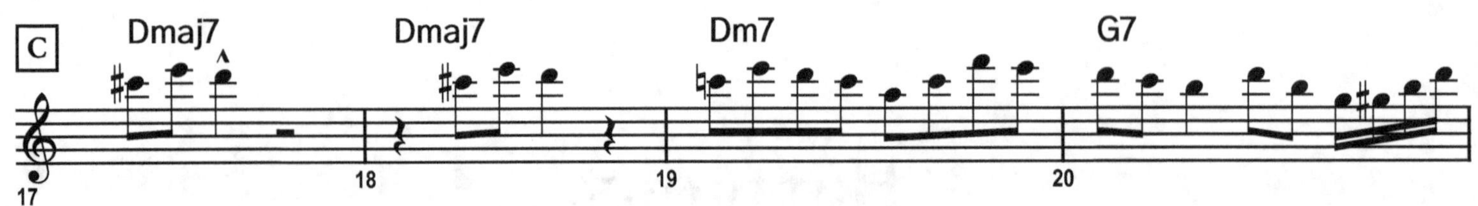

D
Bm7
E7
G♯m7(♭5)
C♯7(♭9)
F♯m7
25
26
27
28
3

B7
Bm7
E7
A6
Em7
A7
29
30
31
32
3
3
3
3

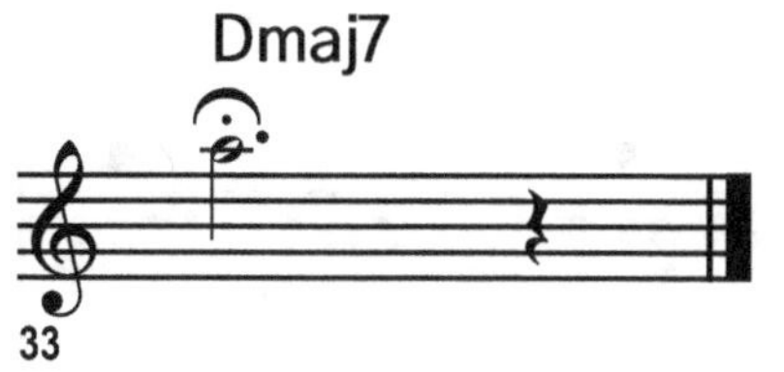
Dmaj7
33

8

MY ROMANCE

JEFF COFFIN

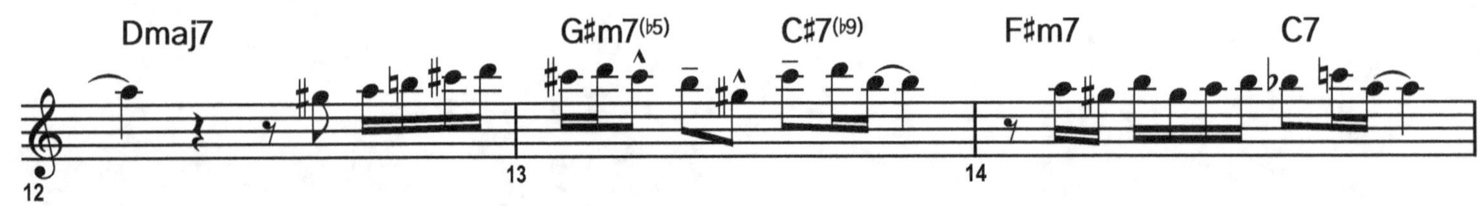

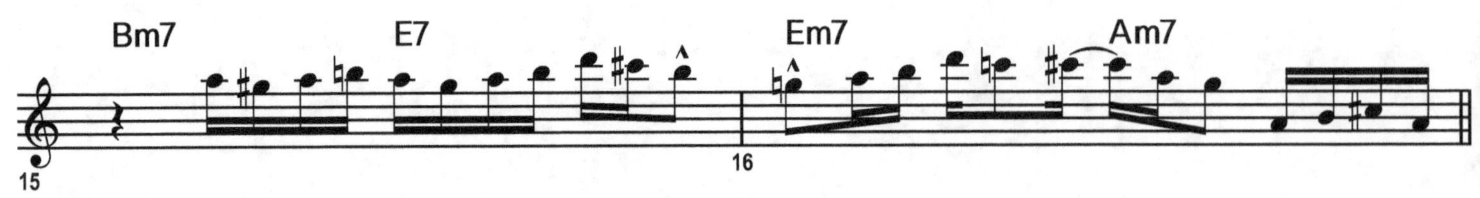

C
Dmaj7
Gmaj7
F♯m7
F∘7
Em7
G♯∘
A7
17
18
19
Dmaj7
F♯7
Bm7
F♯7
Bm7
B7
20
21
22
Em7
A7
Dmaj7
D7
23
24
D
Gmaj7
B7
Em7
/D
C♯m7(♭5)
F♯7
25
26
27
Bm7
B♭7
Dmaj7/A
Bm7
Em7
A7
28
29
30
Dmaj7
Bm7
Em7
A7
Dmaj7
31
32
33

10 LEFT-HANDED IMPROVISATIONAL ETUDES FOR SAXOPHONE

SOPHISTICATED LADY

JEFF COFFIN

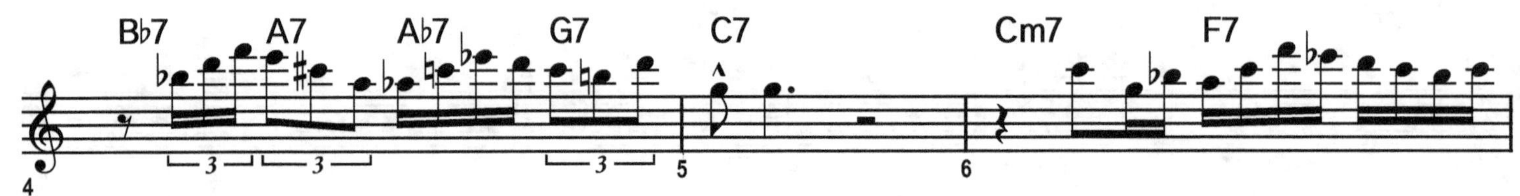

C
Amaj7
F♯m7
Bm7
E7
17
18
3

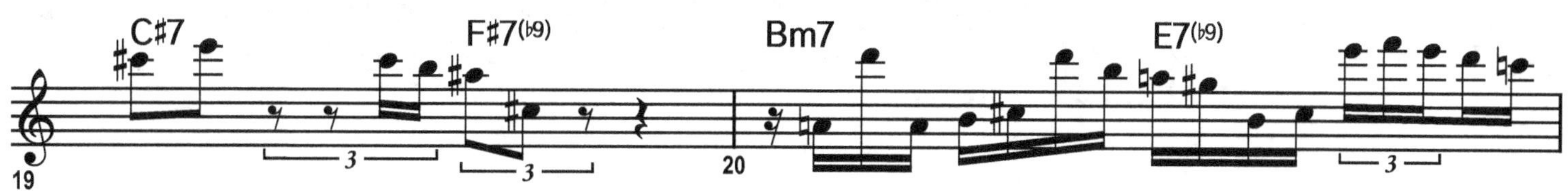
C♯7
F♯7(♭9)
Bm7
E7(♭9)
19
20
3

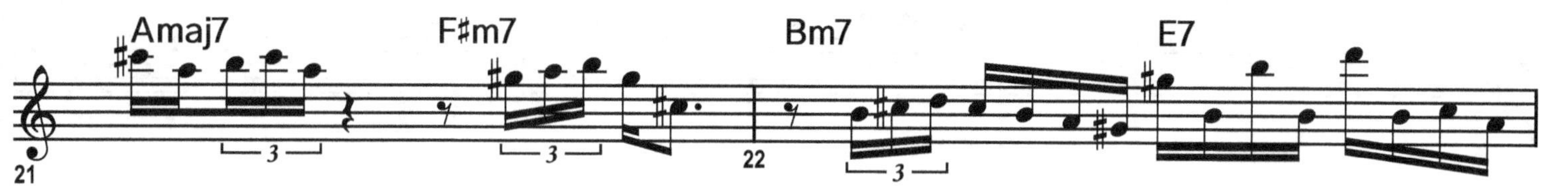
Amaj7
F♯m7
Bm7
E7
21
22
3

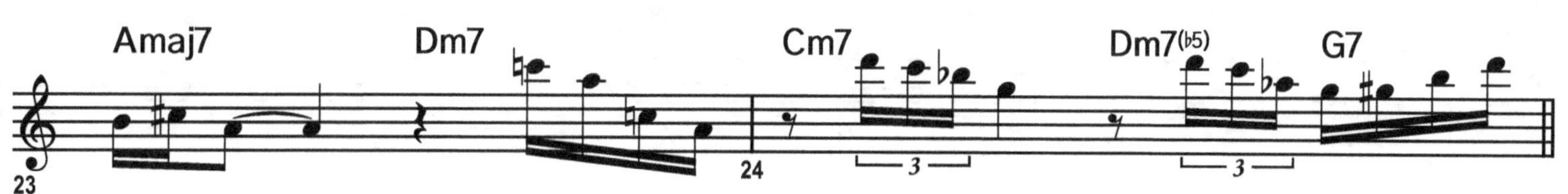
Amaj7
Dm7
Cm7
Dm7(♭5)
G7
23
24
3

D
Cm7
A♭7
C7
G♭7
F7
B♭maj7
25
26
27
3

B♭7
A7
A♭7
G7
C7
Cm7
F7
28
29
30
3

B♭6
Dm7(♭5)
G7(♭9)
Cm7
31
32
33
3

10 LEFT-HANDED IMPROVISATIONAL ETUDES FOR SAXOPHONE

10

THERE IS NO GREATER LOVE

JEFF COFFIN

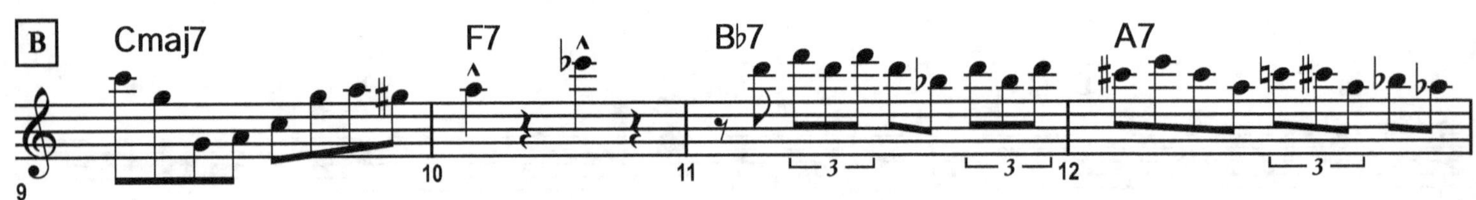

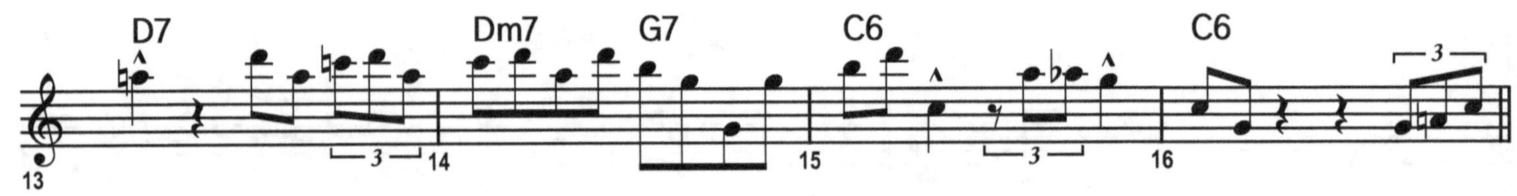

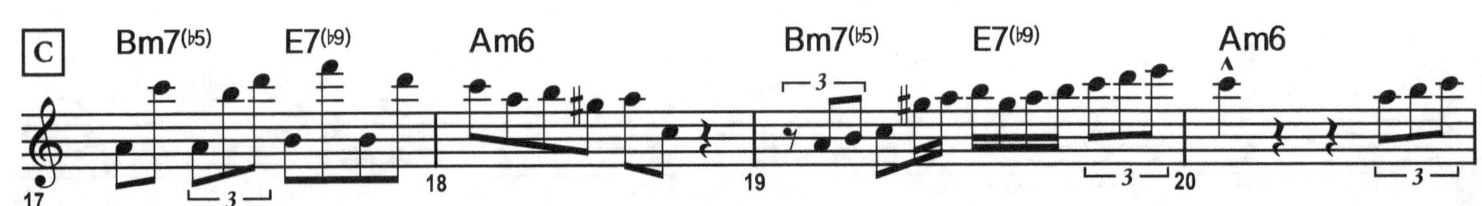

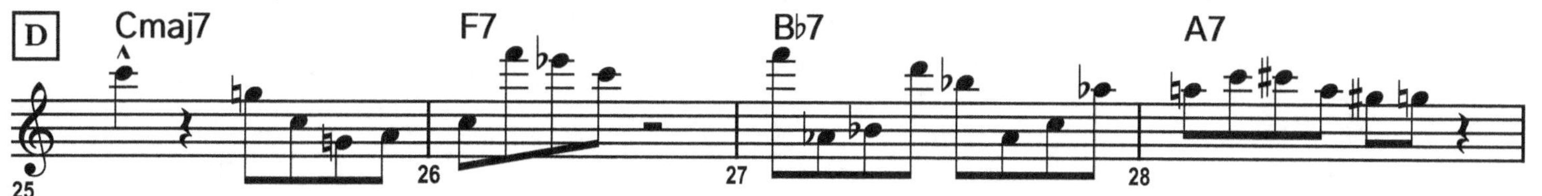
D
Cmaj7
F7
B♭7
A7
25
26
27
28

D7
Dm7
G7
C6
Dm7
G7
Cmaj7
29
30
31
32
33

—

ALSO BY JEFF COFFIN

—

10 Improvisational Etudes
(available for flute, clarinet, alto sax, tenor sax, trumpet, piano, trombone)

The Road Book

The Saxophone Book (1-3)

Jeff Coffin & the Mu'tet Play-Along

The Articulate Jazz Musician (w/Caleb Chapman)

available at www.jeffcoffin.com

www.ingramcontent.com/pod-product-compliance
Lightning Source LLC
Chambersburg PA
CBHW081347120626
46546CB00011B/3471

9781953622174